STORY VINES AND READERS THEATRE:
GETTING STARTED

Marlene McKay

PORTAGE & MAIN PRESS

© 2008 by Marlene McKay

Portage & Main Press acknowledges the financial support of the Government of Canada through the Book Publishing Industry Development Program (BPIDP) for our publishing activities.

All rights reserved. Except as noted, no part of this publication may be reproduced or transmitted in any form or by any means – graphic, electronic, or otherwise – without the prior written permission of the publisher.

Printed and bound in Canada by Kromar.

Library and Archives Canada Cataloguing in Publication

McKay, Marlene, 1952-
    Story vines and readers theatre : getting started / Marlene McKay.

Includes bibliographical references.

ISBN 978-1-55379-155-3

    1. Storytelling—Study and teaching (Elementary). 2. Readers' theater—Study and teaching (Elementary). 3. Language arts (Elementary). 4. English language—Study and teaching (Elementary). I. Title.

PN2081.R4M35 2008   372.6'044   C2008-901602-5

PORTAGE & MAIN PRESS

100 – 318 McDermot Ave.
Winnipeg, MB Canada R3A 0A2
Tel: 204-987-3500 • Toll-free: 1-800-667-9673
Fax-free: 1-866-734-8477
Email: books@pandmpress.com
www.pandmpress.com

FSC
Recycled
Supporting responsible use of forest resources
Cert no. SGC-COC-003098
www.fsc.org
© 1996 Forest Stewardship Council

TABLE OF CONTENTS

INTRODUCTION	1
SECTION I – STORY VINES	3
A Personal Perspective on Story Vines	3
What Is a Story Vine?	5
History of the Story Vine	5
Purposes and Benefits of Story Vines	6
The Process from Start to Finish	9
Assessment	15
A Collaborative Lesson Plan	19
Materials	28
Tips from Teachers	29
Adaptations and Extensions	32
Choosing a Good Story to Model Storytelling	38
Forms and Frames	39
SECTION II – READERS THEATRE	49
A Personal Perspective on Readers Theatre	49
What Is Readers Theatre?	51
Purposes and Benefits of Readers Theatre	51
Getting Started with Readers Theatre	55
Readers Theatre in a Day	62

Texts for Readers Theatre	68
Assessment	69
Writing and Adapting Scripts	70
Adaptations and Extensions	71

FINAL THOUGHTS ON STORY VINES AND READERS THEATRE — 73

REFERENCES — 75

INTRODUCTION

Today's classrooms consist of a wide range of learners. Teachers welcome the challenges of meeting the needs of all learners and developing a supportive, cooperative, inclusive learning community. Story vines and readers theatre are two learning strategies that engage all learners in meaningful literacy learning and provide success. They involve collaboration and cooperation. Students work together to support each other and to problem solve with story and text.

Developing story vines and readers theatre performances requires a series of complex learning tasks. The processes involved in both these strategies are congruent with current and relevant educational theories. The theory of social constructivism, credited to Lev Vygotsky (1934, 1978), the gradual release theory (Pearson and Gallagher 1983), and Cambourne's (1988) eight conditions for learning underlie the success of both story vines and readers theatre. The social constructivist theory of learning posits that learners create or construct knowledge in social situations rather than simply receive knowledge from others. This theory also promotes the idea that learning is grounded in language and that meaning making is a social event. Pearson and Gallagher's theory of gradual release suggests that children will learn from the modelling of others with guided practice and feedback. The ultimate goal of learning is independence, but in order for that to occur, there must be modelling, practice with feedback, and scaffolding for the learners. Cambourne's eight conditions for learning are also key to the success of readers theatre and story vines. Student engagement, along with immersion in language and literacy, demonstrations, expectations of success, increased student responsibility, increased student employment, approximations, and feedback, are essential conditions in both story vines and readers theatre that make them successful instructional approaches.

Both strategies require modelling, setting of criteria, planning and preparation, performance, and reflection and celebration. Both involve much conversation about text, story, author techniques, strategies, literary elements, character, sequence, and events – all the components of text students should think about and explore. Both require students to engage in meaningful contexts and to spend time with the text, rereading, discussing, and analyzing for a purpose. These kinds of activities slow down the process of reading text and therefore help students to understand how texts are constructed and how they work. This helps them to become more skilled readers.

The final performance outcome of story vines and readers theatre differs. Story vines focus on the student's oral presentation of the story or the content, guided and supported by the use of visuals. Readers theatre performances focus on effective and expressive reading of text with the use of minimal props and costumes.

The learning outcomes, goals, and objectives achieved by using story vines and readers theatre with students are similar. Students build confidence in reading, speaking, and presenting in public. They also develop poise. Story vines and readers theatre contribute to the development of a deeper understanding of text and reading strategies, making students more proficient and fluent readers. Both learning strategies lend themselves to many extensions of other language arts learning opportunities. They engage students in critical thinking, problem solving, and cooperative and collaborative learning.

Story vines and readers theatre bring text to life. They make reading and learning fun!

SECTION I
Story Vines

A PERSONAL PERSPECTIVE ON STORY VINES

I always say that you can teach anything if you can find the right story. I love to read books aloud any chance I get, but I found a new pleasure and excitement when I shared my first story vine. I thought that I needed the book to hold and the author's words in front of me to engage my audience in a story. Without the book to read from, I was nervous. But I found a new freedom of expression. I became a storyteller.

I love sharing my vine and engaging the audience with my storytelling. I feel closer to my audience; I am inviting them into the story with my eyes, my body language, my voice, and my vine. Each time I share a story vine, I become more and more confident in my ability to tell the story as if it were my own. I do not have to read the words on the page; therefore, I can connect on a deeper level with the audience. I understand why the planning and sharing of the story vine are so exciting and so much fun for students.

What is a story vine? Can it help students become storytellers? Can story vines enhance language and vocabulary development? Can story vines develop writing ability? Do story vines improve reading comprehension and fluency?

Story vines are a way to make storytelling come alive, to put fun into storytelling, retelling, and oral sharing and presenting. Story vines enhance reading, writing, listening, speaking, representing, and viewing, all the language skills we strive to develop in children. And they are fun!

Sharing my story vine with the students helped me to become a storyteller. I realized that I could engage my audience with the language, body language, the representations on the vine, and my voice and expressions. Here I am telling the story *Something from Nothing*, written by Phoebe Gilman.

Notice the story vines on the whiteboard in the background. These grade 7 and 8 students have made story vines from novels they read. Their vines are long pieces of string and the leaves have been attached to the string along the whiteboard. The leaves tell the story. The students have made very detailed drawings on the leaves.

I see students who are initially hesitant to speak or read in front of anyone become confident storytellers who want to share stories, experiences, and events orally. Story vines work to develop confidence and expertise in storytelling and in all oral presentation skills. Story vines have many advantages for the literacy development of all students. The process of planning and making the vines improves the literacy skills of students of all ages. Hearing stories stimulates the imagination, instills love of language, and motivates students to read and write. Telling stories helps us develop a better understanding of ourselves and the world, as it increases our self-esteem and poise when speaking before an audience.

WHAT IS A STORY VINE?

A story vine is a story visually displayed through representations on a braided vine or rope, held in the hand of the storyteller, and used to tell a story or events. Representations may include objects, pictures, drawings, or any other visual portrayal that strikes the imagination.

A story vine based on the book *Something from Nothing* by Phoebe Gilman.

A series of "prompts" or "representations" are placed along the vine and used as a set of reminders for the storyteller to tell the story sequentially, using the main characters, the main events, and the setting. The prompts or representations help the storyteller to dramatize, as well as to remember the story. The prompts also support the audience's visual appreciation of the story.

HISTORY OF THE STORY VINE

While oral storytelling is a rich part of many cultures, according to the Manitoba storyteller Jamie Oliverio, the story vine originated in Africa.

> *He could see the village from a distance and with each of his long strides, he was a bit closer. The children saw him first and they screamed with delight, shaking the old ones awake and shouting, "He's coming! He's coming!" Now the children surrounded him and the barking dogs and a swirl of dust engulfed them all. He returned each greeting quietly, but their excitement grew.*

He continued walking to the centre of the village, but he stooped to pick up one child and then another in his arms. The day was one of continuous retelling of the news of other places he had visited, but as dusk settled, he began to mark out a circle. At its edge gathered the entire village, seating themselves in hushed silence, waiting their turn.

In the red haze of the sunset, he strode around the circle, and raised his cape, revealing the rough hemp belt and the bright colours of the vines that hung from it. As he stopped in front of an old woman, she reached out and grasped one of the vines. She knew this one, but her gnarled fingers still rubbed each figure lovingly. He took the vine in his hand and began to tell the story. Before the night was done, he had told all the stories, some many times over, and not one of them wished for it to end. And so the storyteller came to the village to tell the stories once more.

— told by Julie Ann Kniskern in a workshop for teachers in Frontier School Division, Manitoba, Canada. Author Unknown.

PURPOSES AND BENEFITS OF STORY VINES

The process of planning, creating, and sharing story vines serves many useful purposes in a classroom and offers many benefits to students (see Figure 1). For example, the process will develop:

- a sense of story and story structure
- comprehension skills (sequencing, summarizing, inferring, evaluating)
- vocabulary and "book talk"
- purposeful rereading
- fluency and pride in storytelling
- oral language
- memory skills
- confidence in reading and speaking
- meaningful connections to characters and events
- integration of language and visual arts
- an understanding of genre
- collaboration and cooperation
- an appreciation of storytelling in different cultures
- an enjoyment of stories and of literature
- confidence in the ability to tell or retell stories, and to speak in front of an audience

THE BENEFITS OF USING STORY VINES

TELLING STORIES USING STORY VINES DEVELOPS...

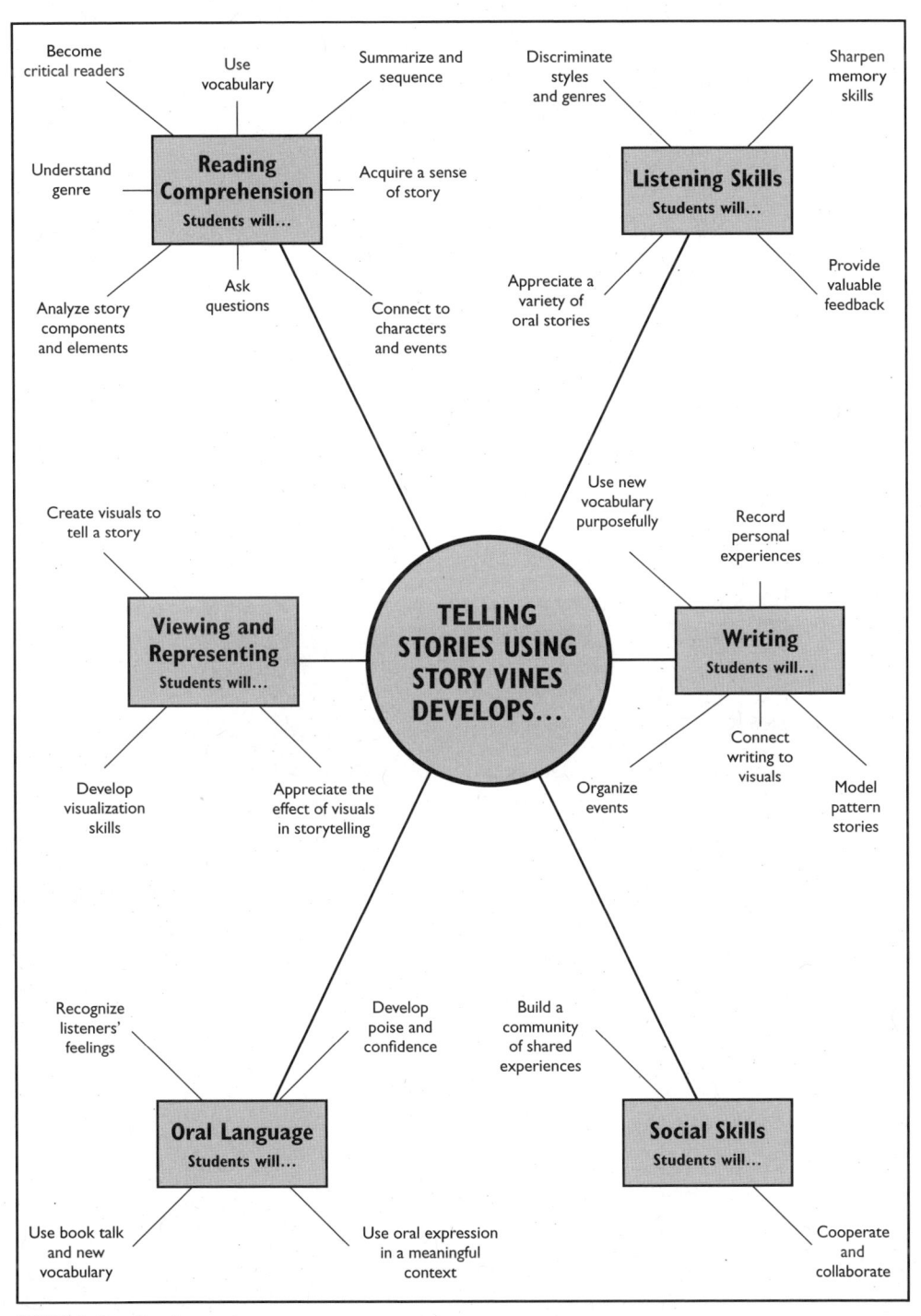

Reading Comprehension
Students will...
- Become critical readers
- Use vocabulary
- Summarize and sequence
- Understand genre
- Acquire a sense of story
- Analyze story components and elements
- Ask questions
- Connect to characters and events

Listening Skills
Students will...
- Discriminate styles and genres
- Sharpen memory skills
- Appreciate a variety of oral stories
- Provide valuable feedback

Writing
Students will...
- Use new vocabulary purposefully
- Record personal experiences
- Organize events
- Connect writing to visuals
- Model pattern stories

Social Skills
Students will...
- Build a community of shared experiences
- Cooperate and collaborate

Oral Language
Students will...
- Develop poise and confidence
- Recognize listeners' feelings
- Use book talk and new vocabulary
- Use oral expression in a meaningful context

Viewing and Representing
Students will...
- Create visuals to tell a story
- Develop visualization skills
- Appreciate the effect of visuals in storytelling

FIGURE 1: Benefits of story vines

This grade 1 student has just finished sharing with her parents at a celebration tea and is very proud to be a storyteller.

THE PROCESS FROM START TO FINISH

A. Modelling:

1. Model what storytelling looks, sounds, and feels like when using a story vine. Show the students how much fun it can be.
   - Invite a storyteller to the class to share the art of storytelling and to model it for the students.
   - Be the storyteller and model the telling of one of your favourite stories using a story vine.

Once the students see how much fun it is and how it is done, they want to do it themselves.

....
Providing a model is a critical first step in engaging the students.
....

2. Discuss the art of storytelling, story structure, and the use of the prompts or representations, and how they assist both the storyteller and the audience.

3. Model the story structure by creating a story map and/or storyboard based on the story that you or the storyteller shared (see Forms and Frames, p. 39). Develop this story map or storyboard collaboratively with the students.

Some students, especially younger ones, should start with a story map. A story map helps students to see the structure of the story and determine the important parts of the story. It can also help students understand the sequence and identify the repetitive language used in the story that may be an important part of the storytelling. Young students often require assistance to understand that stories have a beginning, middle, and end, and that there are important parts to each of these sections.

Figure 2 is an example of a story map created collaboratively with grade 3 students, based on the story *Very Last First Time* by Jan Andrews.

4. Place the story sequence on a storyboard. Some students can use a storyboard without first using a story map. The storyboard helps the students decide on the important parts of the story to be told, and which representations or pictures will go on the story vine. Storyboards may have as few as four or five sections and up to about ten. (See Forms and Frames, p. 39, for different storyboards.)

STORY MAP

Date: _January 16_   Name: _Grade 3 Class_

Story Vine Title: _"Very Last First Time" by Jan Andrews_

CHARACTERS:	SETTING:
Eva and her mother	A village in Ungava Bay in northern Canada. It is in the winter.

BEGINNING:

Eva is getting ready for her very first time to walk on the bottom of the sea alone to gather mussels to eat.

MIDDLE:

Eva and her mother set out, with their mussel pan and ice chisel, across the village to the frozen sea.

MIDDLE:

They shovel away the snow and dig a hole in the ice, and Eva climbs down under the ice onto the floor of the sea. The tide is out so there is no water.

MIDDLE:

Eva fills her pan with mussels and then has time to explore. She finds lots of fascinating sea creatures. Soon she hears the roar of the tide coming in and she is very scared. She jumps and drops her mussel pan and candle, and she cannot see.

END:

Eva searches for another candle, finally lights it, and finds the hole where the moonlight is shining in. She reaches for her mother and climbs out of the sea, and says, "That was my very last first time for walking alone on the bottom of the sea."

FIGURE 2: Sample story map

The model you create collaboratively with the students will be their guide to use for planning their own story.

Storyboard panels:

Eva walks to the sea to get mussels.	They dig a hole to go down under.	Eva fills her pan.
She explores and then hears roar of water.	It is dark Eva is scared.	Eva moms pulls Eva out.

Story Board — Date: Jan 2.
Story Vine Title: Very Last First Time
Student Name: _____

A storyboard from a student based on the story map from *Very Last First Time* by Jan Andrews. This boy will use this storyboard to decide on the representations or pictures that will go on his story vine.

B. Planning and Preparing:

1. Determine which genre to study and share orally (for example, myths, Aboriginal legends of Canada and other countries, folk tales, fairy tales, or just favourite stories). Very young students may use nursery rhymes or very simple fairy tales. (See p. 37 for a picture of a vine used by a nursery class to tell the story of Humpty Dumpty.)

2. Gather a collection of books from the chosen genre. It is important to read some aloud to the class to model the story structure and to teach the genre. Reading aloud also helps the students hear how expression, intonation, pauses, and voices are effectively used in telling a story.

3. Provide opportunities for students to read in pairs and independently from the collection before they decide which story they would like to use for creating their story vines. Story vines may be created individually or in pairs.

4. Students choose the story they wish to share orally.

Section 1: Story Vines

C. Creating the Story Vine:

1. Develop criteria for the retelling of the story: length, number of representations or prompts, importance of sequence, and use of character's words. The elements that you and the students select are important for this storytelling experience will determine the criteria. These criteria may change as you and the students become more experienced and adept at storytelling.

Use these criteria to guide the students and provide feedback as they plan their story vines. These criteria also provide the basis for any assessment you may wish to do.

2. Students chart the main events and characters of their chosen story on a story map or storyboard or both. (See example, p. 26.)

3. Using the storyboard, the students decide which major prompts, representations, pictures, or models are required to support the oral telling of the story and assist the audience. These prompts will be attached to the story vine to create a well-developed and sequenced story.
   - Discuss the prompts or representations that could be used to support the telling of the story and how these representations can be created. These prompts can be simple, such as drawings on a sturdy backing, to elaborate creations from craft supplies or wood. (See p. 28 for ideas on materials to use.)

4. Students decide on genre clues and/or "book talk."
   - Folk tales and fairy tales that begin with "Once upon a time" could start with a clock, for example.
   - Some myths or legends repeat phrases or words. The students may want to represent the repetitions in some way to ensure that they use the word or phrase in the oral telling. For example, in a story I once used as a model, the words "around and around" were repeated in the story. So, on my vine I placed a binder ring to help me to remember to use the phrase "around and around." I used the phrase as I turned the ring around and around to create emphasis. It was effective in helping me remember, but also in engaging the attention of the audience.
   - Some other examples are: a happy face for "happily ever after," a compass or small map for "far, far away," and a map for "in a land far away."

5. Braid the material selected to make the vine. (See p. 28 for tips on braiding and material.)

6. Students use their previously developed storyboard to guide them in the placement of the prompts they will use to tell the story. (See p. 41.)

D. Presenting and Sharing:

1. With the students, develop criteria for oral storytelling. Chart these criteria so that students can practise with the criteria in mind. Students can provide feedback for each other based on the developed criteria as they practise with partners, or you can use these criteria to give feedback to the students. (See Figure 4, Criteria for Storytelling Using Story Vines.)

....

Note that this set of criteria is different and serves a different purpose from the set of criteria developed in step 1 of Creating the Story Vine, opposite page. These criteria will guide the oral presentation. The criteria developed in step 1 are to guide the structuring of the story, and the order and sequence of the vine.

....

2. Practise, practise, practise. Students rehearse their stories, carefully selecting their words, using voices for characters, and using appropriate expression, volume, and intonation. They practise with the criteria that have been developed for oral storytelling. Students need opportunities to practise with a partner and in small groups before they are ready to present to a larger audience. Any feedback during the practice is based on the criteria developed by the students.

3. Record stories on audiotape or videotape as part of the practice so students can hear and/or see themselves and reflect on their own storytelling. Stories may also be taped for others to hear and see. The audiotapes could be placed in a literacy centre with the story vines, so that the listener can follow the story along the vine while listening.

4. Present the story vines to each other, to other classes, to the school, to parents, to elders, and to the community; present to anyone who will enjoy hearing the stories. Students will want to share their stories.

5. Celebrate storytelling and reflect with the students on what you and they have learned and gained from this experience. These reflections will guide what you will change or add when you revisit this process again in your class. Figure 3 provides a summary of the process.

6. Display story vines in the classroom or library.

SUMMARY OF PROCESS

A. MODELLING:

Invite a storyteller.
Be the storyteller and demonstrate the story vine.
Discuss the art of storytelling.
Discuss story structure and the use of a vine.
Model story structure, using the story map and/or storyboard frames.

B. PLANNING AND PREPARING:

Determine the genre to be studied.
Gather books and read aloud.
Allow for time to read individually and in pairs.
Ask students to choose the story to be used.

C. CREATING THE STORY VINE:

Develop criteria for retelling/storytelling.
Chart story on story map and/or storyboard.
Decide on representations/prompts and how to make these.
Determine genre clues and "book talk."
Braid the vine.
Plan and place the representations/prompts.

D. PRESENTING AND SHARING:

Develop criteria for oral presentation.
Practise, practise, practise (in pairs and small groups, with feedback).
Audio- or videotape the performances (optional).
Present and share.
Celebrate and reflect.
Display the story vines.

FIGURE 3: Summary of process

ASSESSMENT

Set assessment criteria during the process of developing the story vines, Identify the skills, strategies, and outcomes you want the students to achieve in this process, and develop criteria with the students based on these. Two important aspects on which to focus assessment are:

1. the structure, sequence, and language of the story. Develop criteria that indicate how well the students understand the genre, the characters, the sequence, the important parts of the story, and the language of the author.

2. the oral storytelling and dramatic aspects of storytelling. Develop criteria to indicate how well the students handle such aspects as:
   - volume, expression, pauses, voices of characters;
   - gestures and use of the representations on the vine to support and dramatize the story; and
   - stance and facial expression.

The criteria become the reference for feedback for learning. These criteria may be simple and few in the beginning and grow and change as you and the students learn more about storytelling and dramatic effects or as you find other uses and adaptations for story vines. (See Adaptations and Extensions, p. 32.)

Students may wish to document experiences and their learning about storytelling in a journal. You will see growth and development in student engagement and confidence through their journal entries.

Developing Assessment Criteria for Oral Storytelling

Planning, developing, and sharing a story vine is a process. Planning, preparation, and practice require a lot of learning, refining, and reflecting. As a group of learners, you will progress, revise, and refine the process as you go along.

The feedback we receive as learners is critical to our continued growth and learning. The feedback for learning and growth is based on the collaboratively developed criteria. A set of criteria upon which to base your assessment and feedback is helpful. Performance is important. Students must know what a successful storytelling performance looks like and sounds like, and they need feedback to continue to improve their performance.

Cathy Miyata (2001) suggests a number of areas that can be assessed to provide feedback for students in increasing their skills and confidence in public speaking. This same set of skills can be adapted with the students to use as criteria for storytelling. The assessment should reflect students' levels of achievement at the time. The criteria will change as you and the students become better and better storytellers.

Figure 4 is a chart that might be used as an assessment guide for criteria. The chart is based on some of the skills suggested by Cathy Miyata (2001) with adaptations based on my classroom experience.

Self-Assessment

The only one who can change the learner is the learner. Self-reflection and self-assessment are important if we wish to grow as learners. Students need to become self-assessors and to reflect on their own learning. Teachers who have used reflections with students are amazed at how the students express what they have learned and what they need to do to grow as learners. I have adapted a self-reflection form, again from the work of Cathy Miyata (2001; Figure 5). Adapt the form to meet the needs of your students.

CRITERIA FOR STORYTELLING

COMMUNICATING IDEAS

    Use of "book talk" or genre cues
    Use of words and vocabulary
    Sentence structure
    Pronunciation

COMPOSURE

    Control
    Posture

AUDIENCE AWARENESS

USE OF EXPRESSION

    Gestures
    Use of vine representations
    Facial expression

USE OF VOICE

    Volume
    Pace
    Use of silence
    Emotional quality

DEVELOPING RAPPORT WITH THE AUDIENCE

    Eye contact
    Audience engagement and participation

OPENING AND CLOSING

OTHER COMMENTS

FIGURE 4: Criteria for storytelling using story vines

STORY VINE PRESENTATION
(self-assessment)

Name of Storyteller: _____ Date: _____
Title of Story Vine: _____

YES	NO		
		Voice:	*Did I speak clearly and with the right pace?*
			Did I speak loudly enough for everyone to hear?
		Story:	*Did I use some of the language of the story?*
			Did I tell the story in sequence with the main parts?
		Composure:	*Did I look calm and in control?*
		Use of vine and gestures:	*Did I use the representations on the vine to enhance my story?*
		Confidence:	*Did I enjoy this experience?*
			Would I like to do this again?

What was the most important thing I learned about myself as a storyteller?

_____
_____
_____

What would I do differently next time?

_____
_____
_____
_____

FIGURE 5: Self-assessment form

A COLLABORATIVE LESSON PLAN

The following is an example of a plan developed collaboratively by a grade 5 teacher and a grade 1 teacher in Manitoba (see Figure 6).

The grade 5 students modelled oral storytelling using a story vine for the grade 1 class.

The following learning sequences are planned using the "Activate, Acquire, and Apply" phases of learning.

Activate: The purpose of this phase of the learning sequence is:
- to access or build prior knowledge and background; and
- to engage the learner and to set them up for a successful learning experience.

Acquire: The purpose of this phase of the learning sequence is:
- to provide modelling, direct instruction, and practice for new learning to occur.

Students require different amounts of time and support to acquire new understanding and knowledge. Differentiation is required, depending on the needs of the learners.

Apply: The purpose of this phase of the learning sequence is:
- to provide an opportunity for students to demonstrate their understanding and show what they have learned.

Grade 5 Learning Sequence

Genre: Legends

Duration: Approximately six weeks

Purposes: To demonstrate an understanding of the legend genre.
To plan and present a story vine through oral storytelling.
To connect language and visual arts.
To demonstrate an increased willingness to share orally.

Processes: Oral storytelling, retelling using visuals, sequencing, oral presentation, and collaborative learning

GRADE 5 LEARNING SEQUENCE

INSTRUCTIONAL LEARNING SEQUENCE	ASSESSMENT
ACTIVATE: Determine what the class knows about legends and how familiar the students are with oral storytelling. **Whole class discussion:** Ask the following kinds of questions to initiate a discussion about legends: • What legends have you heard? • What do you know about legends? • What are the sources of legends? • Why do legends exist? • What messages do they give or what do they teach us? • Why are there different versions of the same legend? Discuss oral storytelling and story vines. Display a braided vine with no story on it.	Determine ongoing formative assessment criteria to match the instructional sequence and to guide the learners. **Does the student:** • have prior knowledge of legends? • understand that legends are a particular genre and have particular features? • take part in the discussions by listening to ideas of others? • participate by adding or sharing ideas or by relevant questions?
ACQUIRE: Modelling: Tell the legend, *How the Chipmunk Got His Stripes*, by using a story vine. Create a gallery walk of the legend books collected from the library and other sources. Allow students to stroll through the gallery in partners to look at the legends and to discuss them. In partners, students choose a legend to be used for retelling. Discuss story sequence with students. • Return to the story told by the teacher. • Model the use of the storyboard. Collaboratively develop the story told by the teacher onto the storyboard. (See The Storyboard, p. 41.)	**Does the student:** • discuss the legends with a partner, by looking at the cover and the titles? • flip through the books to see what further information may be gained? • choose a legend?

INSTRUCTIONAL LEARNING SEQUENCE	ASSESSMENT
• Chart story. • Students read their legends with their partner in order to understand the legend and to become familiar with the sequence and the important events and characters. • Teacher and students develop criteria for the retelling of the legends based on the storyboard developed collaboratively. • Working with their partners, students chart their legends in point form on the storyboard, keeping the ideas in sequence. • Students create images to represent each event in the legend. These images become a set of reminders to help retell the story. Students braid their vines. (See Tips from Teachers, p. 29.) Students place their representations onto the vine.	**Criteria for Storytelling:** • Each story has six to ten events or main parts. • Each main part or event is represented by a picture or image. • The story is in sequence. • Some of the repetitive or cultural language of the author is used in the retelling. • The names of the characters are used. • The title and author are stated. – Developed by the students **Does the student:** • put their story in proper sequence? • match images to events in their story? • use the language of the story (names, places, story language such as "long, long ago," various expressions, etc.)? • follow the criteria? • work effectively with his/her partner?
APPLY: • Develop criteria for oral storytelling with the students. • Chart the criteria for student reference and assessment purposes. • Have partners practise together with their completed story vines, using the criteria for oral storytelling. • Students retell their legends for grade 1 students using their story vines.	**Oral Retelling Criteria:** • Speak loudly enough for the audience to hear you. • Use expression. • Use voices for the characters. • Point to the appropriate representation on the story vine at the appropriate time. • Look like you are having fun! – Developed by grade 5 students **Does the student:** • retell his/her legend according to the oral storytelling criteria?

FIGURE 6: Grade 5 learning sequence

A group of grade 5 students show their story vines outside the class. Their story vines are legends that they read in a genre study unit.

Grade 1 Learning Sequence

This learning sequence follows the model of "Activate, Acquire, Apply" planning format in the same manner as the grade 5 sequence. See Figure 7 for the grade 1 learning sequence and figures 8–11 for examples of storyboards.

Genre: Folk Tales, Fairy Tales, and Nursery Rhymes

Duration: Six weeks, two times a week

Purposes: To connect speaking, reading, and writing.
To enhance student understanding of story structure.
To provide an opportunity for purposeful writing.
To develop oral retelling and understanding of the importance of book talk.

Processes: Attentive listening, retelling, sequencing, collaborative learning, oral presentation

Resources and Materials:
Texts: A variety of fairy tales and nursery rhymes
Resources: Storyboards, story maps
Materials for making the vines: bedsheets cut into lengthwise strips, scrap paper, colouring supplies (markers, crayons, pencil crayons, etc.), scissors, hot-glue gun, small plastic toys, foam pieces, Popsicle sticks, straws, shower-curtain ring

GRADE 1 LEARNING SEQUENCE

INSTRUCTIONAL LEARNING SEQUENCE	ASSESSMENT

ACTIVATE:
 	
The grade 1 class listens to the story vines presented by their grade 5 "care partners."
 	
Through discussion, the grade 1 students set criteria for what good audiences do.
 	
The grade 5 students share their story vines with younger students.
 	
Following the presentations, students discuss the idea of oral storytelling. The students determine the genre.
	Determine ongoing formative assessment criteria to match the instructional sequence and to guide the learners.
	
	Does the student:
	• appear to be listening?
	• sit attentively?
	• watch the presenter?
	• respond to:
	  o the visuals,
	  o the sequences, and
	  o oral language of the storytelling?

ACQUIRE: Have students brainstorm fairy tales and nursery rhymes they know. Record on chart paper. Invite the grade 5 teacher to the class to model his/her story vine. During this modelling, complete a story map on chart paper to show how the story is divided into main parts and has main characters and events. The purpose of this modelling is to introduce the story map and how it shows story structure. Develop criteria with students to guide them in completing the story maps so that they will be able to tell the story using a vine. Ask grade 5 students to assist with the criteria development. Display books of fairy tales and nursery rhymes gathered from the library and other sources. Also display the chart that the students brainstormed about fairy tales and nursery rhymes they knew.	**Criteria for Story Maps:** • Include a beginning. • Include two or three important things that happened in the middle. • Tell the end. • Tell who the main characters are. • Tell where the story takes place. – Developed by grade 1 and 5 students

INSTRUCTIONAL LEARNING SEQUENCE	ASSESSMENT

Have students each choose a fairy tale or nursery rhyme to retell.
 	
A grade 5 student helps review the fairy tale/nursery rhyme by either discussing or reading it to grade 1 student.
	Keep informal anecdotal notes using the following criteria:
	
	Does the student:
	• understand story structure:
	   o beginning,
	   o middle,
	   o end?

A grade 1 student, with grade 5 student's help, completes a story map (grade 1 student prints the words). After completing the story map, the grade 1 student completes a storyboard.	**Does the student:** • stay on task? • use complete sentences when completing the story map and storyboard? • work well with their care partner? • complete the writing task with grade 5 support? • use book talk in written work?
The purpose for using both a story map and a storyboard is so young learners see the story broken into the beginning, middle, and end before they lay out the main events in a sequence for oral retelling. The students used a storyboard frame with eight boxes (see p. 26). Grade 5 students help the grade 1 students braid the material to make the vine. Students create representations for each section on the storyboard to remind them how to tell the story.	**Criteria for Story Maps:** • Use a loud, clear voice. • Recall the sequence of the story. • Use the objects/pictures to help retell the story. – Developed by grade 1 students **Does the student:** • use objects/pictures that visually represent their fairy tale/nursery rhyme? • retell the story in sequence?

INSTRUCTIONAL LEARNING SEQUENCE	ASSESSMENT
• Grade 5 students help grade 1 students create pictures and objects to use on their story vine. • Teacher hot glues the objects/pictures to the story vine with student direction of where each item goes.	Keep informal anecdotal notes using the following criteria. **Does the student:** • use the input from their care partners? • meet the storytelling criteria that were created by the class?
APPLY: The grade 1 students tell their stories to an audience; for example, to their parents or caregivers at an afternoon tea. With the students, develop criteria to guide how to retell the story. • Grade 1 students practise the oral retelling of the story vine with their grade 5 partner, using the pre-established criteria to guide feedback from the students. • Grade 1 students practise their story vine in front of their classmates, using the pre-established criteria. During the family tea, grade 1 students orally retell their story vine to their families. Each child tells his/her story to his/her parent. Display story vines in the school display area.	

FIGURE 7: Grade 1 learning sequence

Story Vine

Goldie locks and the three bears

Characters	Setting forest
Mama bear, Papa bear, baby bear, goldie locks	in the three bears house

Beginning goldie locks finds the three bears house

Middle
1. she eats there porage
2. She sits in their chairs and she broke one.

Middle
4. She finds that the papa bears bead is two hard
5. mamas bed is two soft bb ut baby bears bed is just right and She falls asleep

End
8. The bears come home and there porage has been eaten
9. one of the chairs broke
10. they see her sleeping and she gets scared and runs away

Goldie locks and the 3 bears
by: Hannah and courtney

This is a story map created by a grade 1 student with help from her grade 5 partner. They are using the story map to retell about the character and the events in sequence.

Goldie locks finds the three bears house. No one is home	She eats the le porage.	She sits in there chairs and she broke one	papas bed is to hard
mamas bed is to soft	baby bears bed is just right and she falls asleep in it	The bears come home	they see that Goldielocks is sleeping and she wakes up, gets scared and runs away

This is the storyboard created by the girls, using the previous story map and the book.

Grade 5 students help grade 1 students retell, using a story map to identify the characters and events, and to help them to remember the sequence of the story.

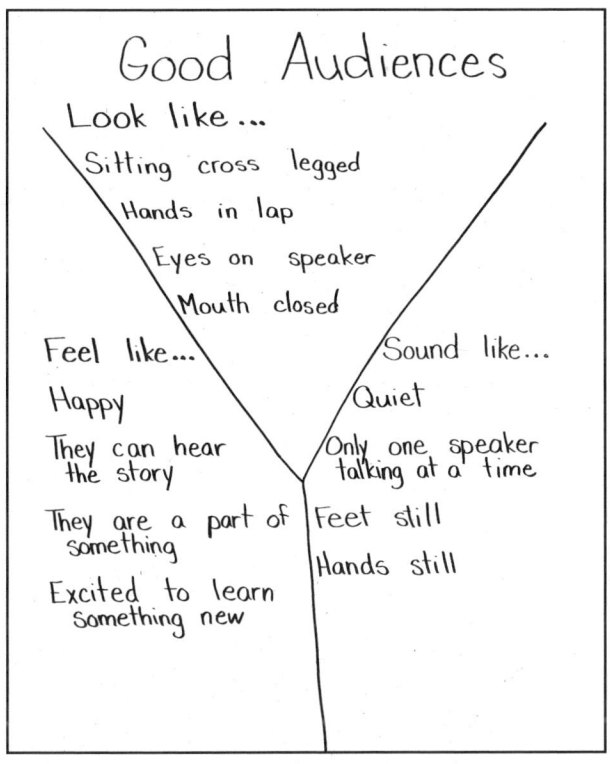

Good Audiences

Look like...
- Sitting cross legged
- Hands in lap
- Eyes on speaker
- Mouth closed

Feel like...
- Happy
- They can hear the story
- They are a part of something
- Excited to learn something new

Sound like...
- Quiet
- Only one speaker talking at a time
- Feet still
- Hands still

The grade 1 class developed criteria on good listening before they listened to the story vines of their grade 5 partners.

27

MATERIALS

Making the Vine

To make the vine, use any materials that can be braided.

If sheets are used, cut the strips 2–3" thick and the length of double or queen sheets. The length is important, because students become frustrated if the vine is too short for their story. If it is too long, students cannot hold onto it and it is awkward to use, which takes away from the storytelling.

The braid has to be wide and long enough to attach the prompts or representations.

Some examples of braiding material:

- yarn (very inexpensive; often most available material)
- sheets cut into strips (durable and easy for young children to braid)
- raffia
- rope or twine
- old nylons
- rug-braiding material
- fabric
- macramé cord

Shower-curtain rings are good to use at the end of the vine. Tie the sheets or braiding material to the ring. Then the ring can be hung from just about anywhere to be braided.

Prompts or Representations

The prompts or representations may be purchased, or made with craft materials. A dollar store is a good place to buy materials for a story vine (e.g., toy farm animals, plastic vegetables). Children's toys also make good icons (e.g., dollhouse furniture).

A wide variety of craft material can be used to create the items to represent the elements of a story:

- felt
- Popsicle sticks
- toothpicks
- buttons
- straws
- fun foam
- pipe cleaners

- fabric
- pompoms
- googly eyes
- construction paper
- yarn
- old nylons and cotton batting (use to make stuffed representations)
- Dough Art (a simple dough that can be shaped and baked in oven)
- cardboard and small boxes
- pictures from magazines
- hand-drawn pictures
- Crayola Model Magic (a modelling clay that can be shaped and left to dry overnight. It can then be easily painted.)
- Styrofoam balls
- old-style clothespins (Add a face and dress them as a character.)
- plastic container lids like those from small yogurt containers (Use yarn for hair and make a face to represent a character.)

A glue gun is a useful tool to attach your representations. You can also tie them onto the vine using string, pipe cleaners, or floral wire, or pin them on using safety pins, clothespins, or paper clips.

TIPS FROM TEACHERS

Making the Vine

If using sheets or other strips of cloth to braid the vine, use two strips of the same colour and one of a different colour. This helps students see how the three strips braid together.

Cut the strips about 2–3" thick. If they are too thin, students find them difficult to braid.

If using yarn, use several strands of yarn for each strand of the braid. This provides some thickness to the finished braid.

Ask for donations of clean, used sheets from local hotels/motels or from parents. Men's ties can also be used.

Younger students require help braiding. Older students can be helpers, or parents or volunteers can make the vines ahead of time.

One teacher had the students physically braid themselves. The shower-curtain ring with the strips was attached to a post. The students wove themselves in and around while holding the ends of the sheets to create the braid.

Attaching the Prompts or Representations

Glue guns work better than white glue or glue sticks. (Laminated pictures will not stick, even with a glue gun.)

If you want to remove the objects, or reuse the vine, do not attach with glue. Attach using pipe cleaners, floral wire, or yarn, or fasten with paper clips, safety pins, or clothespins.

Creating Objects or Pictures

Small toys or objects from the dollar store make great choices for young students.

Have students draw representations on paper and cut them out. They can glue their representations onto Bristol board, cardboard, or foam for more durability.

Encourage the students to use a lot of colour in their representations to engage the audience.

The size of the objects is important. If they are too large, they will not stay on the vine, and if they are too small, the audience cannot see them, and the students have a difficult time using them to assist in the storytelling.

These students are using old sheets to braid their vines. They have two strips of white sheeting and one strip in a blue colour. The ends are attached to a shower-curtain ring.

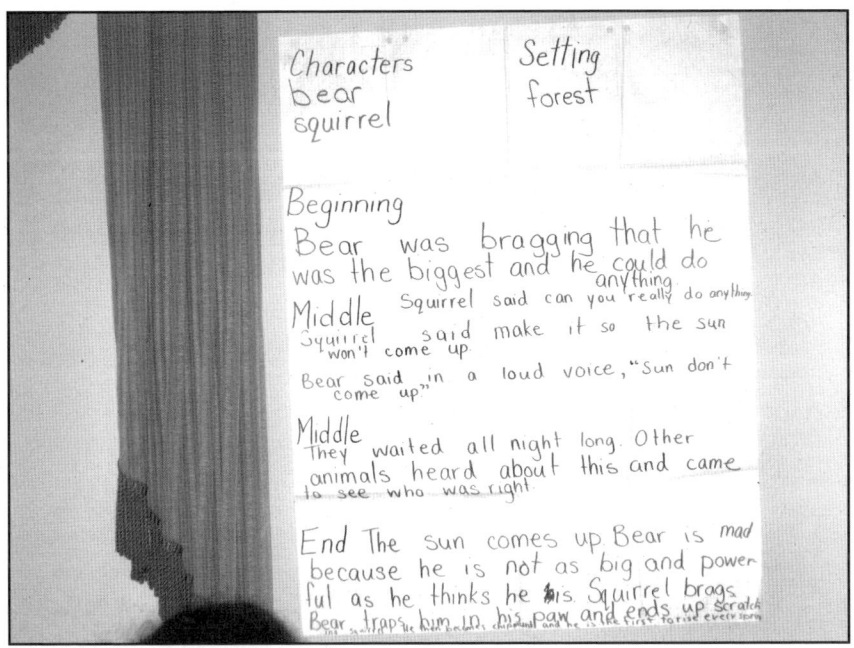

> **Characters**
> bear
> squirrel
>
> **Setting**
> forest
>
> **Beginning**
> Bear was bragging that he was the biggest and he could do anything.
>
> **Middle**
> Squirrel said can you really do anything. Squirrel said make it so the sun won't come up.
> Bear said in a loud voice, "Sun don't come up."
>
> **Middle**
> They waited all night long. Other animals heard about this and came to see who was right.
>
> **End** The sun comes up. Bear is mad because he is not as big and powerful as he thinks he is. Squirrel brags. Bear traps him in his paw and ends up scratching...

As the grade 5 teacher shared his story vine in the grade 1 class, the grade 1 teacher developed the story map of *How the Chipmunk Got His Stripes*. This story map provides the model for the students to do their own story map once they have chosen their book.

Mr. Munroe, a grade 5 teacher, shares his story vine with a group of teachers in a professional development session.

31

ADAPTATIONS AND EXTENSIONS

Most successful processes or strategies can be adapted and extended to meet the needs of the learners. This is also true of story vines. Although the original intent is to tell stories orally using narrative style, there are many other uses for the story vine. It is the process of understanding what goes onto the vine and the practising of the oral sharing that make the story vine successful.

Story Vines in Content Areas

How to's

A story vine works well because sequence is key to the "how to" process. The representations on the vine assist the student in remembering or retelling the steps in a "how to" process. Some examples of content might be science experiments, how to build anything (a rocket, a snowman, a grilled cheese sandwich), how to care for your pet, or how to make a friend.

Recipes

The grade 5 and grade 1 classes that used story vines to tell legends and fairy tales also used the story vines to demonstrate procedural writing. The students made bannock and butter and showed the process of making them using a story vine. Students then each brought a favourite recipe and, using a story vine, told how to make it. The compiled recipe book consists of photographs of the vines that explain the making of the recipes.

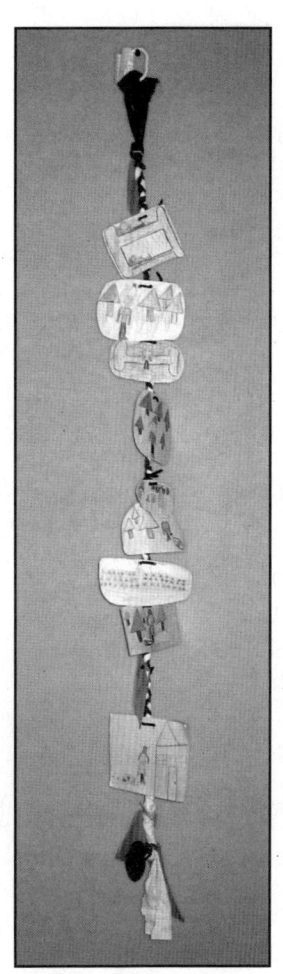

This is an example of a grade 1 story vine. It is hanging from the shower-curtain ring on the wall in the hallway.

History

History can be told as a story in a sequence, and story vines make great prompts to enhance the understanding of the sequence of events in history.

Example: One teacher left teaching and applied for a job as a tour guide for a national park. As part of the interview process, she had to tell the interview panel about the history of the park. Because she had used story vines in her classroom, she used the story vine to tell the park history.

Example: A multi-level grade 3–6 class used story vines to tell the chronological events of Canadian explorers from 986 to 1810. Some pictures of their very elaborate drawings of the events in history are on the following page. The students shared the theme orally, and the vines hung in the classroom as the unit continued.

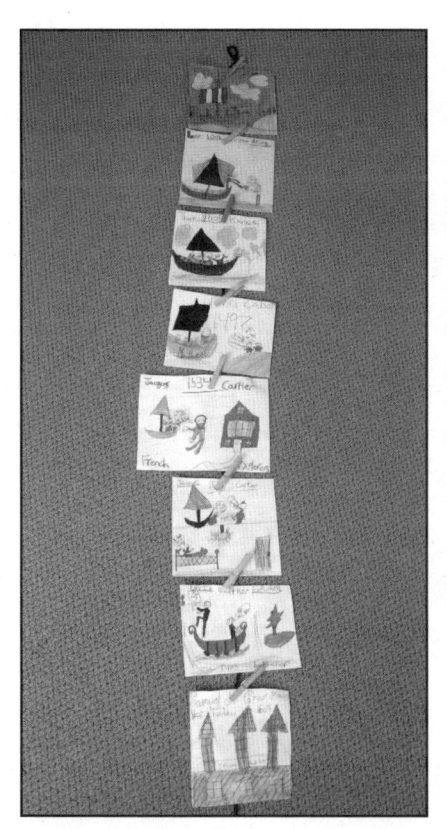

These are two examples of vines that tell the story of historic events in a period of time. These examples are from a multi-level grade 3–6 classroom.

These vines tell the history of explorers in Canadian history. These vines hung in the classroom during the units.

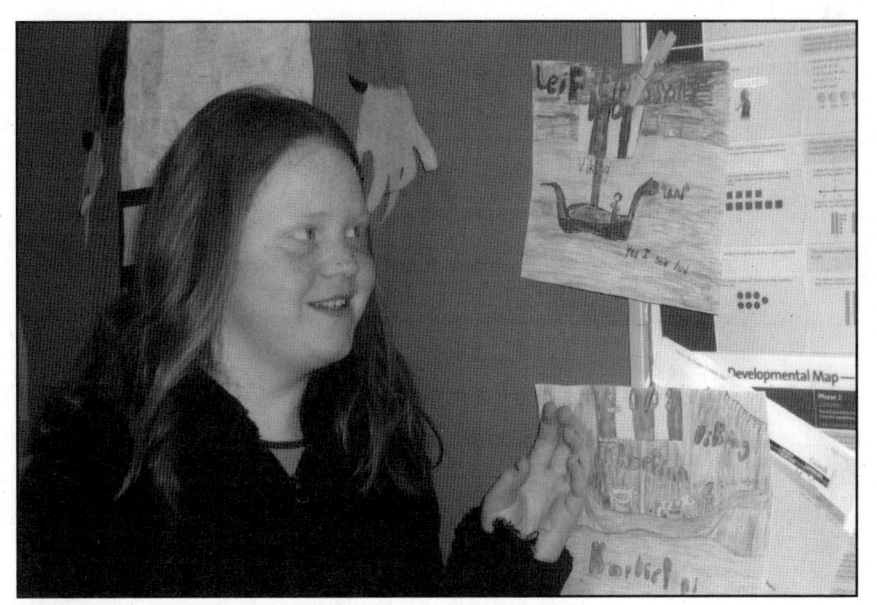

This young student is sharing her vine with the class. She is using the vine to relate historical events in Canadian history.

Biographies

Using story vines to recount the biographies of famous people helps students in planning and remembering the important parts to share. They can share that famous person's life in a memorable and interesting manner.

Field trips or special events

Story vines can be used to recount, in a sequential order, the events from field trips or other special events or occasions.

Story Vines with Info-Fiction or Blended Text

Some books combine narrative fiction with factual information. One class of grade 6 students, working in pairs, made two vines – one for the narrative and one for the factual information. They used these as a tag team, sharing the story and intervening with the factual information. One of the books used was *Salmon Creek* by Annette Le Box. In this book, the story of the life cycle of a salmon is told. The facts are there, but the narrative tells the story from the perspective of the salmon, whose name is Sumi. Another book used was *The Emperor's Egg* by Martin Jenkins. The students shared their vines with students in younger grades.

Story Vines in Literacy Centres in an Early Years Classroom

Listening centre

Audiotape students telling stories with their story vines. Put the audiotape and the vine in the listening centre. Have students follow along on the vine as they listen to the story.

Sequencing centre

Hang vines either lengthwise or crosswise in a centre. Have the students hang pictures of a story onto the vine with clothespins to demonstrate understanding of the story sequence. Vines hang well from chart stands or from hooks on the blackboard, or can be placed horizontally from one corner of the centre to another.

Follow-up to shared reading

After a book has been shared together with a class or small group, students can go to a centre and practise retelling the story using a vine and objects and toys in the centre. The objects can be attached to the vine with pipe cleaners, so they are not permanent.

Place the completed vine in a centre where students can go to retell the story on the vine for practice with oral language and book talk. This is very effective in nursery and kindergarten, when students need to develop language and to learn book talk and vocabulary.

Travelling home story pack

Assemble a story vine, a story, some paper and markers, or objects, or a combination of both. Send the pack home and have parents and students together make the objects for the vine to retell the story. Students return the completed vine to the class to be shared. They then dismantle the vine for the next person to use. The pack rotates to the homes.

Completed story vines could also be sent home and students could retell stories to their parents by using the vine.

Story Vines as Part of an Author Study

Story vines are often used in a genre study, but they can also be part of an author study. There are some authors whose stories are perfect for retelling on a story vine. As the children study the stories of a particular author, they can choose one that they would like to use to plan, create, and present a story vine. Students could work in pairs, small groups, or individually, depending on their age. Some good authors for early years are

This student is sharing her novel vine in her grade 9/10 class.

Helen Lester, Kevin Henkes, and Robert Munsch. A couple of good ones for older students are Patricia Polacco and Eve Bunting.

Story Vines as Family Tree Vines or "All About Me" Vines

Send home materials and a ready-made vine with students so that students and parents can create a story vine about their family. Model this process by sharing a story vine of your family (it can include photos or objects from home). The parents and child can come to class together to share the vine.

You can also have the children make an "All About Me" vine that represents themselves. Model this process by sharing a vine that represents yourself. Use objects, photos, or drawings on the vine.

Story Vines with Novels (Higher Grades)

A group of middle-years students used very elaborate story vines to tell about novels they read in independent reading time. These vines were not braided vines. They were very long pieces of yarn attached to the class whiteboard, with leaf shapes moving along the vine. On each leaf, the students had drawn detailed pictures of each of the main events in their chosen novel. They shared these orally, with the proviso that they would never give away the ending. These vines were displayed in the library after they were removed from the classroom.

This is a vine from a nursery classroom. The students made this with the teacher to retell the story of Humpty Dumpty. The big Styrofoam ball at the top of the vine is Humpty when he is all together. The little cotton balls at the end are Humpty when he can no longer be put back together. The vine is used over and over again in a literacy centre. It helps develop storytelling, sequencing, and use of language for young students.

Story Vines with Original Stories

Students in a grade 6 class made original versions of common folk tales and shared those orally using story vines. They had wonderful versions of *Goldilocks and the Three Bears,* substituting three polar bears and an Inuit hunter. Another adaptation was a hunting and fishing version of *Cinderella.* The students had previous experience sharing stories using vines. Their original text was another way of having the students show their creativity and their stories without a final written draft. Meaningful writing and planning went into these stories in order for the students to share them on a vine. It was a complex process that involved a great deal of writing.

Students in grades 9 and 10 used a complex version of the story vine to tell about novels that they were reading independently. This is a very intricate story that weaves back and forth, and the young storyteller represented that by the use of the yarn to tie the pieces together and to show the complexities of the story.

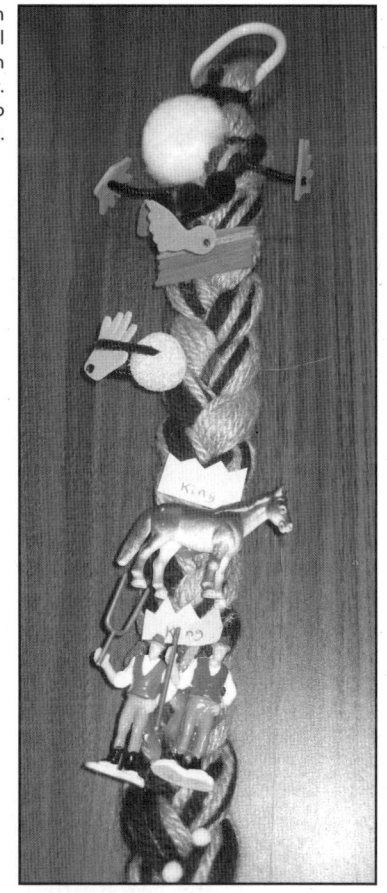

CHOOSING A GOOD STORY TO MODEL STORYTELLING

In choosing a story to share as a story vine, the most important consideration is that you enjoy the story. If you enjoy it, you will enjoy sharing it, and students will enjoy listening and watching as you unfold the story with your vine.

To model storytelling for the students, you should go through the steps of planning and creating your story vine.

Here are a few ideas to consider when choosing a story for a story vine:

- Does the story have a logical sequence of events?
- Is there at least one really interesting or strong character?
- Is there a problem and solution or a decision to be made in the story?
- Is there action in the story?
- Is there some dialogue so that you can incorporate some character voices to add to the storytelling?
- Can the events or character be visualized so that representations can be made and placed on a vine?
- Does the story generate some emotion in the teller and in the audience? Is it funny, sad, scary, or…?
- Do you really like to tell this story?

Suggested Books

We are fortunate that there are so many good books available for children. Those books marked with an asterisk have been particularly successful with middle-years students.

Something from Nothing by Phoebe Gilman

How the Chipmunk Got His Stripes by Joseph Bruhac and James Bruhac

The Wish Wind by Peter Eyvindson

A Story for Bear by Dennis Haseley

Two Pairs of Shoes by Esther Sanderson

Very Last First Time by Jan Andrews

Grandma's Secret by Paulette Bourgeois

A Symphony of Whales by Steve Schuch

Pipaluk and the Whales by John Himmelman

Edward the Emu by Sheena Knowles
Friendship Bay by Deborah Falk
The Gingerbread Girl by Lisa Campbell Ernst
Emma's Eggs by Margriet Ruurs
Nutik, the Wolf Cub by Jean Craighead George
Verdi by Janell Cannon
Big Al by Andrew Clements
*Emma and the Silk Train by Julie Lawson
*Chin Chiang and the Dragon's Dance by Ian Wallace
Omar on Ice by Maryann Kovalski
Don't Need Friends by Carolyn Crimi
*Nanuk Lord of the Ice by Brian J. Heinz
Pumpkin Blanket by Deborah Turney Zagwyn
Suki's Kimono by Chieri Uegaki
The Name Jar by Xangsook Choi
*That's Hockey by David Bouchard
Tulips by Jay O'Callahan
*Dust Bowl by David Booth
Lily's Big Day by Kevin Henkes (and many other books by Kevin Henkes)
Tacky the Penguin by Helen Lester (and many others by Helen Lester)

Blended text (info-fiction)
Salmon Creek by Annette Le Box
The Emperor's Egg by Martin Jenkins

FORMS AND FRAMES

Many forms and frames can help students understand how a story is structured and how they can format the important parts of the story to create a story vine.

Two forms frequently used by teachers are the story map and the storyboard. The following pages show examples of both these frames. These can, as with any good frame or form, be adapted to meet the needs of your students at the time. For example, the storyboard can be changed for very young students so that it has only four frames.

The Story Map

Much of what we read, write, and view is in the form of a story. How often have you been asked to "read a story"? How often do you sit down and share stories with friends or go to the movies to view a "good story"? Children become familiar with narrative from a very early age, and they begin to understand the common elements of a story.

In planning and preparing story vines, it is important that part of what students learn is "what constitutes a story." In learning about the elements and characteristics of stories, students are not only planning and preparing for the making of a story vine, they are also learning about and incorporating story structure. This knowledge of story structure and the elements of story will help students in reading and writing narrative text. Using story maps (Beck and McKeown 1981) is a way for students to analyze the structure of stories and to visualize the elements of the story. This is why using story maps is helpful in planning to tell a story or to make a story vine. The story map helps students to remember the story and makes it easier for them to decide on visual representations to use on the story vine.

Younger students may need to start with a story map. A story map helps students to see the structure of the story and determine the important parts of the story. It also helps students understand the sequence and some of the repetitive language used in the story. The repetitive language may be an important part of the storytelling. Young students often require assistance to understand that stories have a beginning, middle, and end, and that there are some significant parts to each of these sections.

It is important to discuss story structure with the class and to use a simple story as a model to show students how story maps or storyboards work. After modelling a story vine from a simple story of your choice, fill in the story map and/or storyboard with the students so that they can use it as a guide when they do it on their own. Emphasize the recording of the significant events – those events that move the story along.

It is also important to determine the "initiating event" that sets the story in motion. The initiating event is where the story begins. It is the hook for the listening audience. Students should also know about story climax and how that sets up the listener for the ending. This is particularly important for older students who are using more sophisticated stories. Younger students should see that the middle of the story has some important events that lead to the ending, and it is only those important events that we want to tell to the audience.

The story map in this section also outlines the setting and the characters. This is often important for students, and it is why a story map sometimes should precede the storyboard.

The Storyboard

The storyboard is a graphic organizer that helps students determine the main or important events in a story. The way the storyboard is designed also helps the students decide which representations should be used on a story vine to help tell the story. What the storyboard does not have is a place for the students to identify the setting and the characters. If students need help with this, it is best to start with a story map and then move into the storyboard.

Storyboards are often used by cartoonists and film- and videomakers to outline the sequence of important events leading to the climax and ending. In using a storyboard, I often show that the climax box is the second or third box from the end. I sometimes outline that box with a coloured marker so students know that when they get to that box, they should be relating the climax, and that they have only one or two more boxes to bring the story to its conclusion.

Place the story sequence on a storyboard. The storyboard helps the students decide on the important parts of the story that must be told so that the audience will understand and enjoy the story. Storyboards have as few as four or five parts, or up to ten or more. The storyboard is useful for planning how many and which representations are required to tell the story. (See figures 8 to 12 for samples of different storyboards and story maps.)

•••

The model that you create collaboratively with the students will be the guide that they use once they choose and plan their own story.

•••

Story Vine

HUMPTY DUMPTY

Characters	Setting
Kings hourses	outside

Beginning

he was selting on a wall

Middle

Humpty Dumpty fell off the wall

Middle

All the kings hourses and all the kings men tried to put him back together again.

End

But they couldn't put him together again. ANTONINA

This example is from a grade 1 student who used "Humpty Dumpty" as the nursery rhyme he wanted to share as a story vine. He first made the story map (above) and then used the storyboard (below) to plan the sequence of events to represent on the story vine.

Humpty Dumpty	Humpty was sitting on a wall	Humpty then had a great fall	all the kings hourses and all the king men couldn't put him together again
They never put him back together			

42

Story Vine Title: _____

Date: _____ **Student Name:** _____

FIGURE 8: Six-panel storyboard

Story Vine Title: _____

Date: _____ **Student Name:** _____

FIGURE 9: Eight-panel storyboard with rules

Story Vine Title: _____

Date: _____ **Student Name:** _____

FIGURE 10: Eight-panel storyboard

Story Vine Title: _____

Date: _____ **Student Name:** _____

FIGURE 11: Ten-panel storyboard

Story Vine Title: _____

Date: _____ Student Name: _____

CHARACTERS:	SETTING:

BEGINNING:

MIDDLE:

MIDDLE:

MIDDLE:

END:

FIGURE 12: Story map

SECTION II
Readers Theatre

A PERSONAL PERSPECTIVE ON READERS THEATRE

Many years ago, in my second year of teaching, I had a grade 4 class with a wide range of learners. Gordie was in that class. Gordie had fair hair, freckles, and a smile that warmed your heart. He was friendly and outgoing with a charming personality, but he was so discouraged and disappointed every time he tried to read. Gordie had a very difficult time with reading, and consequently also with his self-concept about reading and about language arts in general. I tried to make learning engaging and enjoyable, and though I experienced some success, it was a turning point for all of us in that classroom the day we decided to try readers theatre. A literacy consultant who was visiting our school suggested the strategy to me. He used a ready-made script with the students to explain the readers theatre process. After we tried that script and another ready-made story script, we talked about readers theatre.

As a class, we decided to break into groups, choose a story, practise, and perform it for the rest of the class. Gordie and two other boys chose *Captain Bumble*. The group of boys read the book, delegated parts, practised their parts, made some prompts and a few minimal costumes, and performed it for the others. Theirs was the best readers theater performance in the class. Gordie chose the role of the pirate captain (the most difficult role in the script), and he portrayed the voice and character of that pirate captain in a way that would engage any listener. Gordie excelled in his reading of the text and in his interpretation of the book character. He practised with enjoyment and determination. The performances were a huge success, so much so, in fact, that we decided to invite other classes and our parents to see the performances. Gordie's parents were so pleased and very proud to see him in the front of the class reading with expression, enthusiasm, and passion. Gordon became a reader during that experience. He saw himself as a capable, proficient reader who could entertain an audience by putting emotion into the character of the text. Gordie's transformation was a direct result of participating in readers theatre. He saw himself as a reader, and he was one.

Since that day, I have used readers theatre over and over and over again, and always with success. I see Gordie every time I work with a group or a class on readers theatre. I see Gordie in every hesitant student who becomes a more competent and confident reader in a short time, using readers theatre. I am so grateful that I was introduced to readers theatre early in my career. It worked for me and for my students and it can work for you and your students. I use readers theatre consistently year after year to make reading come alive for readers of all ages.

Readers theatre is not an end in and of itself. It is a means to engage learners in meaningful reading, writing, listening, speaking, viewing and representing, and cooperation. Readers theatre is a vehicle to teach the skills and strategies of language arts to all students. The performance is important, but the process that gets the students to that performance is where so much learning takes place.

Readers theatre is for everyone. It is an inclusive approach that engages all the readers in the class – the most proficient, the somewhat proficient, the discouraged, the struggling, the ones with English as an additional language. Everyone gets the opportunity to read with passion and pleasure and to take on different roles and characters.

This group of students from a multi-level class in Matheson Island School is performing a readers theatre script called *The Crow's Potlatch*.

Some of the characters in the readers theatre performance of *The Crow's Potlatch*.

Readers theatre can be practised and performed with fiction and nonfiction and at any grade level. It is fun, easy to prepare and execute in any classroom, and it engages students in reading the way we often wish they would.

WHAT IS READERS THEATRE?

Readers theatre involves students reading aloud from scripts, with minimal props, sets, or costumes. The emphasis is on oral expression and interpretation of the text.

Readers theatre can be as simple as a shared reading of a nursery rhyme, poem, favourite text, or picture book, or as complex as adapting and writing scripts for a reading performance.

Readers theatre engages readers of all ages; it makes reading fun; it brings text to life.

PURPOSES AND BENEFITS OF READERS THEATRE

Readers theatre can be used to improve:

- oral reading, fluency, and accuracy
- comprehension skills – reading for deeper meaning, making meaningful connections to characters and events
- purposeful use of a repertoire of reading strategies
- self-monitoring of reading strategies

- writing skills
- listening skills
- confidence and poise
- collaborative and cooperative learning skills

and to encourage:

- retelling and sharing of stories
- enjoyment of literature and appreciation of drama
- performance in front of others
- use of language and vocabulary
- risk taking
- active engagement in the reading process (reading, rereading, thinking, rethinking, and responding and reacting to what has been read)

Readers theatre requires students to understand or make meaning of the original text as they decide which parts will be in the voice of the various characters, which parts will be delivered by a narrator, and where shifts in mood, tone, character, feelings, and events take place. In doing that, students begin to understand how stories and text are constructed; they begin to attend more to the techniques and elements that authors use. This kind of analysis of the text is the most valuable aspect of the teaching and learning. The preparation of a readers theatre script and performance from their own or another's text slows down the time students spend engaged in the text. We know that time-on-task is a most significant element in learning.

This class is performing the script *The Elves and the Shoemaker*.

Telling Stories Using Readers Theatre Develops...

Reading Comprehension
Students will...
- Become critical readers
- Understand vocabulary in a meaningful context
- Learn dialogue and sequence
- Understand genre
- Acquire a sense of story
- Analyze story components and elements
- Ask questions
- Connect to characters and events

Listening Skills
Students will...
- Discriminate styles and genres
- Sharpen memory skills
- Appreciate a variety of oral stories
- Provide valuable feedback

Viewing and Representing
Students will...
- Create visuals to tell a story
- Develop visualization skills
- Appreciate the effect of visuals in storytelling

Writing
Students will...
- Use new vocabulary purposefully
- Record personal experiences
- Understand dialogue and conversation
- Understand voice in reading and writing
- Model pattern stories

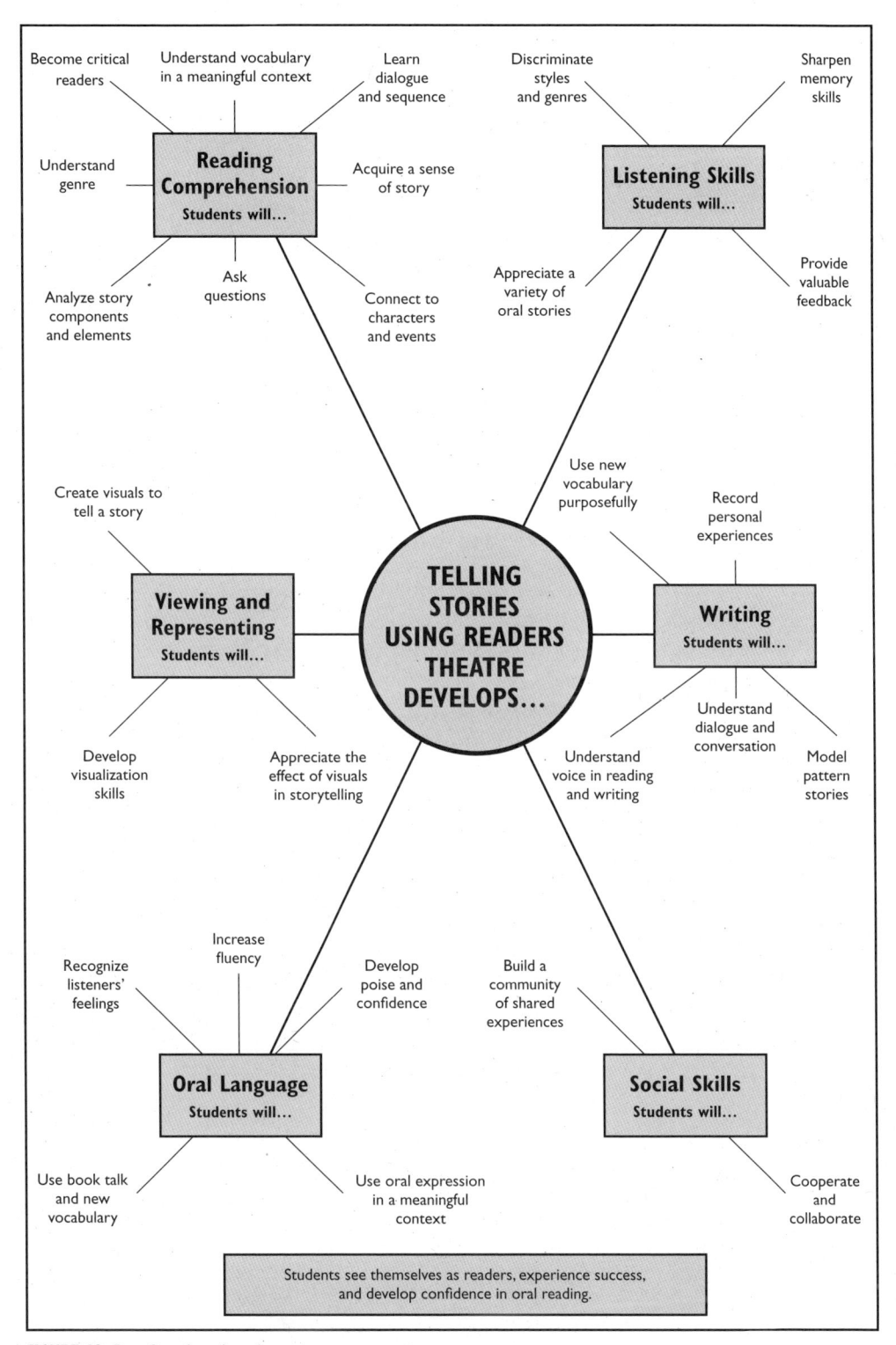

Oral Language
Students will...
- Recognize listeners' feelings
- Increase fluency
- Develop poise and confidence
- Use book talk and new vocabulary
- Use oral expression in a meaningful context

Social Skills
Students will...
- Build a community of shared experiences
- Cooperate and collaborate

Students see themselves as readers, experience success, and develop confidence in oral reading.

FIGURE 13: Benefits of readers theatre

Many useful resources are available that suggest different ways of introducing and using readers theatre with students. No single method suits everyone. As with any good strategy or process, make adaptations based on the needs of your students and your situation.

The steps suggested in this section for introducing readers theatre in a classroom are based on the gradual release of responsibility and the model of explicit instruction (Pearson and Gallagher 1983). In this model, responsibility for learning is gradually released to the student. Teachers have responsibility for explicit teaching and modelling. As teaching and learning continue, teachers provide opportunities for practice with ongoing feedback for improvement. As students become familiar and comfortable with the process, the skills, and the strategy, they assume more of the responsibility for learning with less guidance and support. The teacher monitors the students' progress and continues to provide feedback. The period of guided practice and the level of support vary for each student. The goal is for students to apply the skills, knowledge, and experience independently and to direct their own learning.

The following steps are a suggestion for introducing readers theatre to students. They are based on the gradual release of responsibility and my experience with using readers theatre in a variety of classrooms with a wide range of learners. Also underlying the success of readers theatre is the theory of social constructivism, which posits that learners construct meaning in social situations and use language as a meaning-making tool. As well, readers theatre incorporates Cambourne's (1988) eight conditions for learning: student engagement, immersion in language and literacy, demonstrations, expectations of success, increased student responsibility, increased student employment, approximations, and feedback.

GETTING STARTED WITH READERS THEATRE

A. Modelling:

1. Find suitable text for readers theatre. Consider:
   - interest of the students
   - quality of the language
   - features of the text – repetition, cumulative structure, humour
   - amount of dialogue (more is better)
   - quality of the plot (should be strong and fast-moving)

2. Read the text aloud to the students.
   - Introduce the text to the students and explain any difficult concepts or vocabulary.
   - Read the text in its entirety so students have the sense of the story, poem, or script.
   - Read with fluency and lots of expression – the students need to hear the dialogue and the characterization modelled. It is important to provide a model of what good reading sounds like. Use different voices for different characters to add to the reading.

B. Planning for a Presentation:

1. Discuss the characters in the script or story.

Discuss the characters with the students. Ask what they think the characters are like, based on your reading of the story. Students can begin to analyze the characters, what characters say and do, and what they might be thinking or planning. Discuss the author's intent or theme. Point out how the characters' feelings and voices change during the story. Perhaps they are afraid in the beginning and then they are excited or happy or relieved at the end. Discuss how the voice, expression, intonation, and volume may change as the feelings or circumstances in the story change. Ask: Why do you think the characters acted the way they did? How do you know what they were feeling?

2. Chart the characters.

Make a chart of the characters. The chart may also include information such as the connections among the characters and their relationship to each other. This helps the students to visualize the characters and their relationships.

3. Decide on narration roles and characters.

Once the characters have been charted, discuss the parts in the story that were not spoken by anyone but are necessary for the audience to understand what is happening in the story. These parts become the narrator parts. List narrator/s on the chart with the characters. The chart is now a chart of Roles and Characters. See the following sample (Figure 14) of a chart of Roles and Characters based on Phoebe Gilman's *Pirate Pearl*.

It is important for students to discuss and examine the role of the narrator and that of the characters, and how those roles differ. The distinction between the roles affects the drama, pace, and flow. Discuss why some information can be narrated, but other information should be given by a character.

The number of different characters in the text and how many narrator parts are required determine how many readers are required for each performance. There can be any number of narrator parts, depending on how many students you want to work together with any given text.

Pirate Pearl by Phoebe Gilman

Roles and Characters
Princess Pearl – lead character who lives with the pirates
Captain Plunk – pirate captain who finds Pearl in the sea
Macaroone – teaches Pearl how to act like a pirate
Prince Basil – searches for the missing princess
Count Crumple – evil count who tries to get rid of Princess Pearl to take the throne
Narrators

FIGURE 14: Roles and Characters chart

4. Assign roles to students.

Assign each student or group of students the role of narrator or character. You can allow students to choose their role or character. It can be surprising to see which roles particular students will choose. It is then important for them to experience success by being encouraged or assisted in that reading.

5. Develop the script and practise the role or character.

Provide a copy of the text for each assigned role and character. Students highlight with coloured highlighters the dialogue of their particular assigned role or character.

It is important to have a discussion about dialogue and the use of quotation marks. It is also important to talk about the phrases "he said," "she answered," etc. These are not part of the dialogue and, in readers theatre, these phrases are not highlighted and are not spoken in the reading. The reader reads the character as if he or she were that character.

On completion, there will be highlighted scripts for each character and narrator part.

Label the front of the script or copy of the story with the part that is highlighted. For example, if the narrator is highlighted, that script or book is labelled "Narrator." That copy is then the script for that particular role or character.

You can also write scripts on chart paper or on an overhead projector so students do not have to hold the script and can be free to use hand movements and mime. Colour-code the various characters and roles so that students can find them easily.

Read through the script. Allow students to ask questions, make comments, or react to the story. Discuss voice projection, intonation, good vocal expression, facial expression, and gestures.

6. Change roles and characters, and practise (optional).

Students can choose any one of the scripts to practise that character or role, in partners, small groups, or individually. Place the scripts in a learning centre where students can practise rereading, choosing different roles or characters each time.

C. Presenting and Sharing:

1. Decide on minimal props and costumes that may be used in the performance.

Costumes and props are not necessary. The reading is the important part. However, students often want to add to their character and to the dramatic effect by adding simple costumes or props, such as hats, whiskers, glasses, a piece of relevant equipment, or a sign to tell the time of day. Costumes and props help some students to "get into character" and be less nervous about reading or performing. Whatever props or costumes are chosen, students should be able to make or find them easily so the performance can take place.

2. Practise, practise, practise.

Students need time to practise their role or character, in small groups, in partners, or with the teacher. To ensure that practice time is meaningful and guides improvement, develop some criteria of the expectations of oral reading in a readers theatre presentation. Criteria may be set in a number of ways (see Figure 15). Some classes build a Y chart like the one on the following page. They discuss what readers theatre should look like, sound like, and feel like. These criteria become the basis of the feedback during practice as well as the assessment criteria for the students and teacher.

3. Provide feedback for improvement.

When practising, students benefit from feedback on their reading and their interpretation of the character or role. Feedback is provided by the teacher or by other students, based on the discussion of the character and the reading of the text, and the criteria set with the students.

4. Perform.

In a readers theatre performance, it is preferable if students can sit on revolving stools on a stage or in the front or centre of the room. Characters may turn in and out of a scene when not involved. Readers turn around to exit or enter.

Usually, however, schools do not have revolving stools, so chairs can be placed at the front of the room in either a line or a semi-circle. Students can help decide on the most strategic manner of placing the characters and the narrators. If there are two central characters who interact and converse with each other, they are often placed either in the centre or perhaps one on each end. The other characters are then strategically placed around them. Narrators are often at the ends. Sometimes, the narrator is off to the side or behind slightly. Narrators sometimes stand and characters sit.

Each student has a script, and they read for their script in a dramatic and expressive manner. The scripts are usually put into binders, Duo-Tang covers, or simple file folders so that all the fronts look the same from the audience's view.

The audience watches and listens. Most of the enjoyment for the audience is in the variation in the voices and the interpretation of the characters by each of the readers.

Students can perform in front of each other, or invite other classes, parents, and others to see the performance.

5. Celebrate and reflect.

Students need an opportunity to reflect on their performance. They also need an opportunity to celebrate oral reading and presentation. Remember that they are risk taking in front of others and they need to feel successful. Figure 16 is a form (adapted from Miyata 2001) that could be used for self-assessment. It can be changed and modified to match the criteria that were developed with the class.

Criteria for Reading Reader's Theater

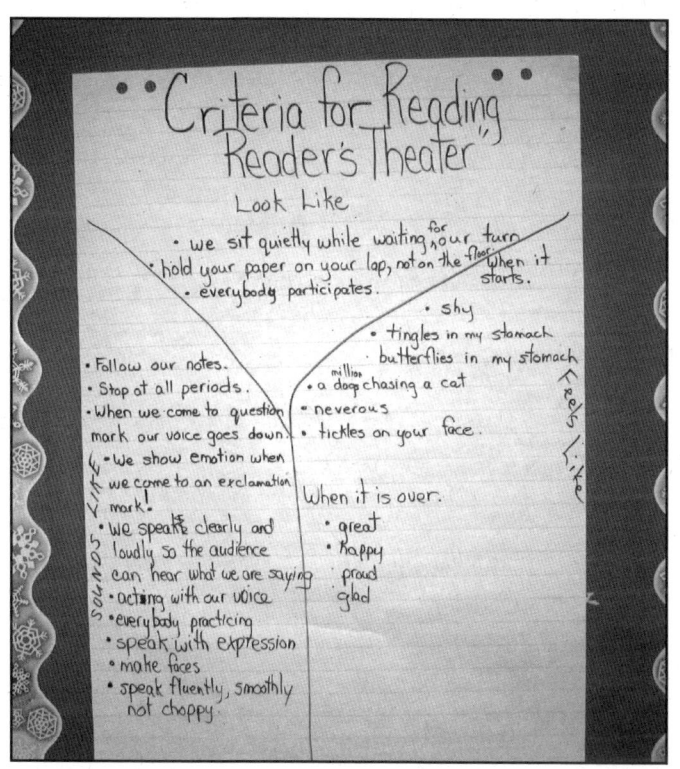

Look Like
- we sit quietly while waiting for our turn
- hold your paper on your lap, not on the floor when it starts.
- everybody participates.

Sounds Like
- Follow our notes.
- Stop at all periods.
- When we come to question mark our voice goes down.
- We show emotion when we come to an exclamation mark.
- We speak clearly and loudly so the audience can hear what we are saying
- acting with our voice
- everybody practicing
- speak with expression
- make faces
- speak fluently, smoothly not choppy.

Feels Like
- shy
- tingles in my stomach
- butterflies in my stomach
- a million deep chasing a cat
- neverous
- tickles on your face.

When it is over.
- great
- happy
- proud
- glad

Y-chart with the criteria for readers theatre. This was built collaboratively with students in a K–4 class.

Criteria may also be in the form of a list.

What Makes a Good Readers Theatre Presentation?

- Feeling like the character or role you are reading
- Reading with expression and emotion
- Reading loudly enough for everyone to hear
- Following along so the reading flows
- Holding your folder/script so the audience can see your facial expressions
- Pausing at appropriate times
- Reading with the right pace (not too slow but not too fast — just the way the character would talk)
- Making readers theatre look enjoyable and easy

FIGURE 15: Criteria of a good readers theatre presentation, developed by grade 6 students

READERS THEATRE PRESENTATION
(self-assessment)

| Title of script: _____ | Date: _____ |

Name of reader: _____ Character or role: _____

YES	NO		
		Voice:	*Did I speak clearly and with the right expression?* *Did I speak loudly enough for everyone to hear?*
		Character or role:	*Did I sound like the character or the narrator?* *Did I make that character come alive for the audience?*
		Use of facial and/or body expression:	*Did my facial or body expressions add to the character or role I was reading?*
		Confidence:	*Did I enjoy this experience?* *Would I like to do this again?*

What was the most important thing I learned about oral reading?
_____
_____
_____

What would I do differently next time?
_____
_____
_____
_____

FIGURE 16: Self-assessment form

SUMMARY OF STEPS FOR INTRODUCING READERS THEATRE

A. MODELLING:

Find a suitable script or text for readers theatre.

Read the text aloud to the students so they understand the story.

B. PLANNING FOR A PRESENTATION:

Discuss the characters in the script or story.

Chart the characters.

Decide on narration roles and characters.

Assign roles to students.

Develop the script and practise the role or character.

Change roles and characters, and practise (optional).

C. PRESENTING AND SHARING:

Decide on any minimal props or costumes that may be used in the presentation (optional).

Practise, practise, practise.

Provide feedback for improvement.

Perform.

Celebrate and reflect.

FIGURE 17: Summary of steps

READERS THEATRE IN A DAY

This is a sample of a learning sequence that was used in a multi-level classroom to introduce readers theatre. This class is in a small, remote community, and it is a one-teacher school with students ranging from nursery to grade 9.

Sample Learning Sequence

The following learning sequence is planned using the "Activate, Acquire, and Apply" phases of learning (Before, During, and After).

Activate (Before): The purpose of this phase of the learning sequence is:
- to access or build prior knowledge and background; and
- to engage the learner and to set them up for a successful learning experience.

Acquire (During): The purpose of this phase of the learning sequence is:
- to provide modelling, direct instruction, and practice for students to acquire new knowledge, skills, strategies, and experience. Students require different amounts of support and different amounts of time to acquire new understanding and knowledge. Differentiation is required, depending on the needs of the learners.

Apply (After): The purpose of this phase of the learning sequence is:
- to provide an opportunity for students to demonstrate their understanding and show what they have learned about readers theatre, reading aloud, and cooperation.

Topic: Readers Theatre

Grade: Multi-level classroom, grades 1–9

Purposes: To engage the entire classroom in a cooperative reading activity.
To support and encourage reading aloud for all grades.
To introduce readers theatre.

Processes: Read aloud, rereading with a purpose, cooperative group learning, oral presentation

Text chosen: *Pirate Pearl* by Phoebe Gilman (picture book)

This is a lively story with lots of dialogue and humour. The story is about a young princess who is set out to sea in a treasure chest as a baby by the evil Count Crumple. She is discovered by pirates who take her under their care and teach her the swashbuckling ways of a pirate's life. Pirate Pearl learns to steal treasure, but she gives it away to those in need. Unknown to Pearl and the pirates, there is a reward offered for Princess Pearl's safe return and of course a young prince attempts to earn that reward.

MULTI-GRADE LEARNING SEQUENCE

INSTRUCTIONAL LEARNING SEQUENCE	ASSESSMENT
ACTIVATE: The book chosen for modelling is a picture book called *Pirate Pearl* by Phoebe Gilman. Discuss the title and author of the story and show the front and back cover. Discuss what students know about the life of pirates. Talk about what this story might include, considering the title and the cover pictures. Before you begin to read, set a purpose for listening. Tell the students that you are going to read a story and that they are to listen for enjoyment and for what the pirates do and say in this story. They are also to listen to discover how many characters there are in this story and decide which character they think is the most interesting and why. **First Reading:** Following the first reading of the story, discuss the story and the characters. Discuss how the characters felt and how this is shown. Talk about why the characters acted the way they did. Make a chart on chart paper of all the characters in the story. Tell the class that they will do a readers theatre with the story and that all of them will be taking part. Discuss what readers theatre might look like, sound like, and feel like. Record the responses on a large Y chart.	Assessment is ongoing and formative. Does the student: • have any prior knowledge or experience with pirates and stories about pirates? • listen attentively? • appear engaged in the story? Does the student: • identify the characters? • tell which character was interesting and provide a relevant explanation? Does the student: • contribute to the discussion about readers theatre? • appear to have some understanding of what readers theatre might look like, sound like, and feel like?

INSTRUCTIONAL LEARNING SEQUENCE	ASSESSMENT
	What does readers theatre Look like? Sound like? Feel like?
ACQUIRE: Reread the story. This time, stop in various places to discuss the characters and how the story could be presented in a readers theatre. (You may choose to have this story on an overhead for the students to see the dialogue and the punctuation, especially the quotation marks.) Stop after the second page, because there is no dialogue until the end of the second page. It is important to introduce the idea of narrator. Discuss and decide which parts should be narrator and which parts should be delivered by the characters. Add the narrator to the chart of characters. Continue with the rereading, stopping at various points to discuss the voice of the characters and the role of the narrator. Discuss how the phrases "she said," "he asked," and so on, are not part of the dialogue and, like in a play, you do not read them. You read *as if* you are the character. Explain the use of quotation marks. With the class, set some criteria on what a good oral reading presentation looks like and sounds like. These criteria are used to provide feedback during practice sessions.	Does the student: • engage in the discussion with relevant ideas and opinions? Recognize which students require some instruction, guidance, and support in rereading the text and highlighting to make a script. Make informal observations as you work with the small groups. Does the student: • read the text easily or need support? • understand the different characters and use of dialogue? • reread with the purpose of determining the role and dialogue of their assigned character? Does the student: • reread with accuracy and expression? • maintain the voice of the character? • use the criteria and feedback based on that criteria for improvement?

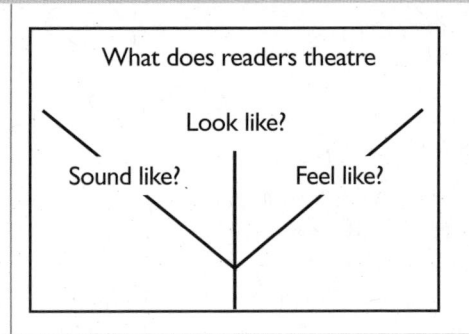

INSTRUCTIONAL LEARNING SEQUENCE	ASSESSMENT
Following the second reading of the book, tell the students that they are going to make a script for each of the characters and roles. This class decided on one narrator. In this class, because it is multi-level, we divided the students into pairs of an older, more proficient reader and a younger, less proficient reader. We gave each pair a copy of the book and a coloured highlighter, and asked them to reread very carefully and highlight the words that their assigned character or role will read during the performance. After students complete the scripts, check to ensure accuracy. Discuss how this story will look as a performance. The class decided that the older students will perform the readers theatre. The three grade 1 students were assigned two tasks: 1) finding or making the props and costumes; and 2) helping the older students practise to ensure that they sounded and appeared like the character they were assigned. The younger students were aware of the criteria for the oral reading. Ask the older students to choose their role and practise with the grade 1 partner or in pairs with another character.	
APPLY: Discuss the format of the readers theatre and the need for a few minimal props and costumes. The grade 1 students planned and prepared the costumes and props.	**Does the student:** • look for appropriate costumes and props that demonstrate understanding of the characters and the story?

INSTRUCTIONAL LEARNING SEQUENCE	ASSESSMENT
All the props and costumes came from the Play Box in the school. Students chose a pirate hat, a string of pearls, a lady's hat, an eye patch, a crown, a box that resembles a treasure chest, and other small articles.	
Students decided on the arrangement of chairs and the placement of the characters and the narrators. They practised the performance several times on the arranged chairs. The teachers and students provided feedback during the practice sessions.	**Does the student:** • arrange the chairs to support the dialogue and interactions in the story? • work cooperatively with the others? • provide feedback using the pre-determined criteria?
The students performed the readers theatre for the nursery and kindergarten students and parents.	
Following the performance, we celebrated with a healthy treat. The following day, the older students were asked to write a reflective journal piece on their performance and what they would like to try next as a readers theatre. The younger students were already choosing books that they would like to perform as a readers theatre. Their choices ranged from some simple fairy tales to their favourite books.	

FIGURE 18: Multi-grade learning sequence

The chart of characters and roles for the book *Pirate Pearl* by Phoebe Gilman was developed with the students after the first reading.

This is the grand performance of *Pirate Pearl* by students in Stevenson Island School.

TEXTS FOR READERS THEATRE

Ready-Made Scripts

Scripts are readily available already adapted or written with the speaking parts and narrator roles provided. They are easy to use and generally can be reproduced so that every student has a copy. Ready-made scripts are a great way to introduce readers theatre.

There is a wonderful script on page 9 of the book *Learning with Readers Theatre* by Neill Dixon, Anne Davies, and Colleen Politano (1996). This script introduces the concept of readers theatre to a class. It is called "Introducing Readers Theatre" and is designed for three readers.

Winn Braun and Carl Braun have a number of books available that have scripts for all ages (see References). They provide a wide variety of scripts ranging from simple rhymes to complex scripts with several characters.

Children's Picture Books

There are many wonderful children's picture books on the market, which are excellent for readers theatre because they are well written and meant to be shared and enjoyed aloud. Good quality literature introduces students to new vocabulary and language, characters, and situations that they can read and enjoy in context. Most good quality children's books require little if any adaptation to become a readers theatre script. Choose children's literature that has strong characters and plenty of dialogue. Children love humour, and they love books where the characters are doing funny things.

The following are a few of my favourite books to introduce readers theatre.

Pirate Pearl by Phoebe Gilman

Paper Bag Princess by Robert Munsch

Clara Caterpillar by Pamela Duncan Edwards

Tacky the Penguin by Helen Lester

Chin Chang and the Dragon's Dance by Ian Wallace

Rattletrap Car by Phyllis Root

Don't Need Friends by Carolyn Crimi

Emma's Eggs by Margriet Ruurs

The Christmas Orange by Don Gillmor (We did this one as a staff at a Christmas reading in the library.)

Big Chickens by Leslie Belakowski

The Fourth Little Pig by Teresa Celsi

The following three books are about reading and can help introduce some reading strategies and the value of reading, as well as readers theatre.

Wolf by Becky Bloom

Henry and the Buccaneer Bunnies by Carolyn Crimi

Book, Book, Book by Deborah Brass

ASSESSMENT

Assessment of students engaged in readers theatre is an ongoing process for both teachers and students.

Key pieces in the assessment process are:

- modelling by the teacher
- setting criteria with the students
- observing and providing feedback
- self-assessing and reflecting on learning

Modelling sets the example from which students build criteria. Reading aloud and having other good readers read aloud to students gives them the opportunity to see and hear what good reading is like.

Setting and using criteria tell the students what is important in the task and what they are to strive towards in their practice. The feedback that we receive as learners is critical to our growth and learning. Performance is important, and students need to know what successful readers theatre performances look like and sound like. They also need feedback in order to continue to improve their performance. Decide which skills, strategies, or outcomes you want the students to achieve in this process and develop criteria based on these. Two important aspects on which to focus assessment are:

1. the oral reading. Develop criteria that indicate how well the students read orally. This may include narrative expression, interpretation of character, volume, facial expression, gestures, pace, use of pauses for dramatic effect, etc.

2. cooperative and collaborative learning. Readers theatre is meant to be a shared activity. The success of the performance depends on cooperation and collaboration. It is important to discuss this with the students, and you may wish to set some criteria for this as well. Students need to reflect on the importance of working together and knowing that a performance is a team effort.

The criteria become the reference for feedback for learning. These criteria may be simple and few in the beginning, and grow and change as you and the students learn more about readers theatre, oral reading, dramatic effects, and working together. The criteria may also change if you find ways to adapt readers theatre to use in content areas (see p. 72).

Students may wish to document experiences about readers theatre and working together. As they develop confidence and expertise, they can reflect on their learning through journal entries. You will also see growth and development in student engagement and confidence through their journal entries.

WRITING AND ADAPTING SCRIPTS

After using ready-made scripts and children's books that require little adaptation, students often want to write their own scripts. They can adapt fairy tales and other stories for a script, or write original scripts. If the students have experienced readers theatre using either ready-made scripts or children's literature, they will have a good model for what a readers theatre script is like.

Steps for writing scripts:

1. Ensure that students recognize story structure and sequence:
   - beginning – introduction of characters and setting
   - problem – some problem occurs
   - minor resolution – problem appears to be solved
   - complication or new problem
   - ending or resolution

2. Show the format of a script:
   - name of character or role on left side
   - character name in bold

3. Plan and write a script together.

Use a story map or storyboard (see section 1, pp. 39–42, for information on story maps and storyboards) to plan the sequence of the story. Storyboards are very useful for planning as they have a set number of spaces and the students know where the climax and resolution appear on the board.

Choose a short story or fairy tale to demonstrate how it can be adapted to a script. Write the script together, discussing important aspects as you proceed. This script will provide a model for students if they choose to write their own.

Scripts are better when written in small groups or pairs. As students discuss the story, structure and dialogue are formed. Students also develop a deeper understanding of the story and the characters through discussion and problem solving. Readers theatre is a cooperative activity.

ADAPTATIONS AND EXTENSIONS

Readers theatre, like any good instructional strategy or process, can be adapted to meet the needs of your students. Here are a few suggestions.

Adapting Novels as Readers Theatre

Older students can choose sections or chapters of a novel, then write or use dialogue from the novel and perform readers theatre.

Developing a readers theatre on a chapter read early in the novel can also help students to better understand the characters and deepen their understanding for further reading.

Using Poetry or Nursery Rhymes with Young Children

Young children can use various lines or parts of a poem or nursery rhyme to perform readers theatre.

Using Readers Theatre as Follow-up in a Literacy Centre

Scripts or children's literature can be placed in a literacy centre. Students can read various parts and record themselves. They can listen to the recordings and reread to improve their oral reading skills.

Using Readers Theatre in an Author Study

Certain authors have written several books or stories that lend themselves well to readers theatre, because they have lots of interesting dialogue and humour, and are about issues and concerns to which students relate. Some authors to use for an author study that would include readers theatre are Helen Lester, Kevin Henkes, Robert Munsch, Phoebe Gilman, Paulette Bourgeois and the Franklin series, and Stan and Jan Berenstain and the Berenstain Bears series.

A grade 2 teacher wanted to introduce and incorporate readers theatre into her class. It was getting close to December, and that school held a concert for parents each December. This teacher also wanted to integrate education about character virtues. She decided to have her students read Franklin books with the idea that they would adapt and perform these books for readers theatre. The students were also to decide which character virtue was prevalent in the book of their choice. The class first went through the process together. The teacher provided much modelling and direct instruction (gradual release of responsibility). The class performed and videotaped the first collaborative readers theatre. After they watched their performance, the students developed criteria based on what they did well and what they wanted to improve upon in their next performance. The teacher divided the students into groups. Each group read, discussed, and analyzed several Franklin books, then chose the one they wanted to adapt, practise, and perform. At the concert, each group performed their readers theatre with few props and costumes and some great reading. Following each performance, the students displayed a large sign that showed the character virtue they learned about in that particular story (for example, honesty, respect, responsibility, and empathy). These character virtues, with the name of the book from the Franklin series printed on the page, were displayed in the hall for a few weeks after the performances.

Using Readers Theatre in Content Areas

History

Students can write and perform scripts based on people and situations in history. Select an historical event, then write and read aloud conversations that would occur during that time period.

Science

Students can write scripts to explain scientific discoveries, properties, or relationships. Characters and roles can be scientists, reporters, or interviewers wanting to find out about discoveries or the facts about something in science.

Nonfiction picture books

There are many wonderful nonfiction picture books. Students can share the information in the text in a readers theatre performance. One grade 3 class used the books of Gail Gibbons. These texts have information in various formats. Students were divided into groups of four. Each group chose a text (for example, *Owls* by Gail Gibbons). The students had to decide how to break up the text for reading and how to include in a performance the different ways the information was presented. They also decided on minimal props, some of which were diagrams. They performed the readers theatre for each other. By the time the unit was finished, they were experts not only on their topic, but also on the reading of nonfiction text.

FINAL THOUGHTS
on Story Vines and Readers Theatre

Learning is a social activity, and students continue to construct and reconstruct their own identity through literary practices. Our role as teachers is to provide meaningful learning opportunities that encourage students to think critically and work collaboratively. It is important for students to be immersed in language, to take risks, to receive constructive feedback, and to become engaged in literacy learning.

Story vines and readers theatre presentations are inclusive instructional approaches that engage all learners in listening, speaking, reading, writing, viewing, and representing in an integrated manner. Students achieve many learning outcomes or objectives. Students work together to comprehend and respond to text. They critically examine text and construct meaning through interaction and discussion with others. Fluency is enhanced as well as social and cooperative learning skills. Listening and speaking are improved and students gain a greater appreciation of literature. Students demonstrate increased confidence in reading and speaking.

The added element of performance, presentation, or sharing gives the students a real purpose for engaging in the learning. Students learn in many different ways, and readers theatre and story vines encourage learning through visual, oral, and tactile experiences.

I have witnessed the many benefits of using both readers theatre and story vines with all ages. I truly hope this book has given you a reason for trying either or both of these exciting and successful approaches.

REFERENCES

Beck, I., and M. McKeown. "Developing Questions that Promote Comprehension; The Story Map." *Language Arts* (1981): 913–918.

Braun, Winn, and Carl Braun. *Readers Theatre: More Scripted Rhymes and Rhythms*. Winnipeg, MB: Portage & Main Press, 1995.

———. *Readers Theatre: Scripted Rhymes and Rhythms*. Winnipeg, MB: Portage & Main Press, 1995.

———. *A Readers Theatre Treasury of Stories*. Winnipeg, MB: Portage & Main Press, 1996.

———. *Readers Theatre for Young Children*. Winnipeg, MB: Portage & Main Press, 1998.

———. *Readers Theatre in Rhyme: A Collection of Scripted Folktales*. Winnipeg, MB: Portage & Main Press, 2005.

Buehl, Doug. *Classroom Strategies for Interactive Learning*. Schofeld, WI: Wisconsin State Reading Association, 1995.

Cambourne, B.L. *The Whole Story: Natural Learning and the Acquisition of Literacy*. Auckland, New Zealand: Ashton-Scholastic, 1988.

Dixon, Neill, Anne Davies, and Colleen Politano. *Learning with Readers Theatre*. Winnipeg, MB: Peguis Publishers, 1996.

Gregory, Kathleen, Caren Cameron, and Anne Davies. *Setting and Using Criteria*. Courtenay, BC: Connections Publishing, 1997.

Hill, Susan. *Readers Theatre: Performing the Text*. Armadale, Australia: EC Publishing, 1990.

Manitoba Education and Training. *Kindergarten to Grade 4 English Language Arts: Manitoba Curriculum of Outcomes and Grade 3 Standards.* Winnipeg, MB: The Author, 1998.

Miyata, Cathy. *Speaking Rules.* Markham, ON: Pembroke Publishers, 2001.

Pearson, P. David, and Margaret C. Gallagher. "The Instruction of Reading Comprehension." *Contemporary Educational Psychology* 8 (1983): 317–344.

Pellowski, Anne. *The Story Vine: A Source Book of Unusual and Easy to Tell Stories from Around the World.* New York, NY: Macmillan, 1984.

Sheperd, Aaron. *Readers Onstage.* <www.aaronshep.com/rt/index.html.> Accessed February 2, 2007.

Vygotsky, L. *Mind in Society: The Development of Higher Psychological Processes.* Trans. M. Cole, V. John-Steiner, S. Scribner, and E. Souberman. Reprint, New York, NY: Cambridge University Press, 1978.